Songs of
Ancient
Journeys

Songs of Ancient Journeys

Animals in Rock Art

Elsa Marston

GEORGE BRAZILLER PUBLISHERS

New York

Published in 2005 by George Braziller, Inc.

Text copyright © 2005 by Elsa Marston

Photographs copyright © 2005 by Doak Heyser, Wes Holden, J. Q. Jacobs, Peter Krocek, and Ray Rasmussen

For information, please address the publisher:

George Braziller, Inc.

171 Madison Avenue

New York, NY 10016

Library of Congress Cataloging-in-Publication Data:

Marston, Elsa.

Songs of ancient journeys : animals in rock art / by Elsa Marston. -- 1st ed.

p. cm.

ISBN 0-8076-1558-7 (hardback) -- ISBN 0-8076-1563-3 (pbk.)

1. Indians of North America--Southwest, New--Antiquities. 2. Petroglyphs--Southwest, New. 3. Rock paintings--Southwest, New. 4. Animals in art. 5. Decoration and ornament--Animal forms--Southwest, New. 6. Southwest, New--Antiquities. I. Title.

E78.S7M325 2005

709'.01'130979--dc22

2005018734

Design by Jeffrey J. Faville

Printed and bound in Singapore

First edition

PHOTOGRAPHS

Page 2: *Newspaper Rock,* Utah; photograph by Ray Rasmussen. Page 8: *Hunting Panel,* Nine-Mile Canyon, Utah; photograph by Doak Heyser. Page 12: *Snake,* South Mountain, Arizona; photograph by Peter Krocek. Page 14: *Bighorn Sheep,* Kane's Creek Canyon, Utah; photograph by Doak Heyser. Page 17: *Ducks,* Canyon del Muerto, Canyon de Chelly, Arizona; photograph by J. Q. Jacobs. Page 19: *Mountain Lion,* Three Rivers Petroglyph National Recreation Site, New Mexico; photograph by Wes Holden. Page 20: *Turtle,* Three Rivers Petroglyph National Recreation Site, New Mexico; photograph by Wes Holden. Page 23: *Lizard,* South Mountain, Arizona; photograph by Peter Krocek. Page 25: *Butterfly,* Willow Springs, Arizona; photograph by J. Q. Jacobs. Page 27: *Bison,* Shay Canyon, Utah; photograph by Ray Rasmussen. Page 29: *Elk,* Perry Mesa, Arizona; photograph by Peter Krocek. Page 31: *Bear Print,* Montezuma Canyon, Utah; photograph by Doak Heyser. Page 32: *Deer,* South Mountain, Arizona; photograph by Peter Krocek. Page 35: *Rabbit, Harvest Panel,* Maze District, Canyonlands National Park, Utah; photograph by Ray Rasmussen. Page 37: *Dog,* Temple Mountain, San Rafael Reef, Utah; photograph by Doak Heyser. Page 38: *Hand Prints,* Needles District, Canyonlands National Park, Utah; photograph by Ray Rasmussen.

For Savannah,
who will write her own songs one day,
with my love

With thanks to Polly Schaafsma
for introducing me to the
fascination of seeing rock art "in the wild"

Introduction

EVER SINCE PEOPLE FIRST THOUGHT of making their marks in the world, they have used rock surfaces to convey messages. Nowhere is this more evident than in the American Southwest, where humans began creating images on rock more than 8,000 years ago. These images were made either by scratching or chipping away the surface (petroglyphs), or by "painting," applying pigment to the rock face (pictographs). Today, just to have a convenient term, we call both petroglyphs and pictographs "rock art." But were these images "art" to those who made them—or something altogether different?

Many symbols and images in Southwestern rock art appear to have been concerned with hunting, encouraging plentiful game and success in the hunt. Others were apparently intended to promote fertility: rain, good crops, and healthy babies. Many of the most intriguing were probably related to the activities of shamans—individuals believed to have magical powers and the ability to help their people by traveling to the spirit world and communicating with the spirits. Rock art figures that suggest humans changing shape, for instance, are sometimes explained as representing shamanic activity.

Most people who study Southwestern rock art, however, agree that interpreting the signs with any degree of certainty is virtually impossible. The images were probably used for a variety of purposes—identifying clans, marking trails, recording important events. Other rock images seem to have been associated with religious ideas, rituals, or magic intended to affect nature. At most rock art sites there are no other clues—for instance, legends or archaeological finds—that might help explain the signs. The cultures of historical Indian groups, such as Pueblo peoples and Utes, may suggest some ideas; but trying to interpret rock art is still mainly guesswork.

The inspiration for this book came from a trip I made a few years ago to study rock art in southeastern Utah. Many sites can be viewed easily. Other rock art, however, is found in places that are difficult and dangerous to reach—cliffsides, overhangs, or caves high on a canyon wall. Those sites were probably believed to have special sacred power; thus, the images must have had a significance quite different from that of signs easily seen by anyone passing by.

For me, the greatest fascination of rock art comes from a feeling of awe: we are standing in the same spot where someone stood long ago to make marks on stone, probably for some very serious purpose. We can't know what was in that person's mind—yet we can feel a connection over hundreds, even thousands, of years.

Figures of animals are what I find most appealing in rock art. In the traditional world of Native Americans, animals and humans were partners of equal importance. Animals were thought to have magical powers that could affect the lives of humans. Shamans seem to have had special relationships with animals; much rock art may have been intended to enable shamans—with the assistance of certain animals—to enter the spirit world.

In my poems, I decided to let the various animals speak for

themselves, as they move through their daily lives. Movement is, in fact, the connecting theme. Even though most animal figures in Southwestern rock art appear stiff and static, it seems to me that their continuing appeal, over so much time, implies a form of motion . . . a journey from then to now. This book will affirm a link, I hope, between our lives and those of the people long ago whose rock art inspires our own imaginations today . . . because we are all inheritors—and guardians—of this wonderful planet.

Snake

Silent as sunlight,
Smooth as slickrock,
I slip through the grass,
Swerve over sand,
Slither on stone,
Slide among shadows.

Sere leaves and pebbles
rustle and whisper
Secret songs as I pass.

Because my course is
Sideways and sinuous,
never straightforward,
never direct,
Some say I'm stealthy,
Seclusive and sly,
Subtle and singular,
not one to trust.

But I'm bound to the Mother
closest of all.
Of all her children,
I'm always in touch.

Bighorn Sheep

         up!
    up,
Up,

Up the sheer cliffs
to the highest crags!
Each hoof finding the perch-point it needs—
        no matter how sharp
        or crumbly the ledge—
to the top of the world, to the edge of the sun,
my nimble feet lift me as light as the breeze.

Down,
        down,
            down!

Off the high peaks
through the thin, clear air,
with barely a glimpse at the rocks below—
        no leap too far
        or chasm too deep—
to the lush green meadow besprinkled with flowers,
my winged hooves bear me with elegant ease.

Duck

My walk is a waddle,
a dawdle, a plod . . .
my swim just a paddle,
aimless and odd.

To dive I turn bottom
up, tail to the sky.
If I knew a better way,
surely I'd try.

I flap my wings hard when
I take to the skies—
for me, fancy flying
would hardly be wise.

No, I'm not much to look at,
ungainly and stout.
A laughable figure,
I wander about
on water, or under,
on land and in air . . .

but that's just the point—
I can go ANYWHERE!

Mountain Lion

Low to earth I prowl through the pines,
gliding from patch of light to shade.
Like falling needles my paws make no sound,
but mark my passing in fresh-drifted snow.

> *Be warned, be wary as I draw near . . .*
> *silent as mist, stealthy as nightfall.*

Out on a ledge, beneath winter's sun,
crouching, I gaze far over my realm.
No creature stirs on the crags below—
above, no birdcall my presence betrays.

> *Be warned, be wary, for I am still here . . .*
> *silent as mist, quiet as dewfall.*

I watch, unmoving, as shadows grow deep . . .
I wait till the right moment comes

> *to leap!*

Turtle

One foot,
                two foot,
three foot,
                four . . .

That's my speed,
                that's it, no more.

Moving a house takes lots of thought,
and careful planning for each new spot,
with constant watching to see the humps
and skillful steering to miss the bumps.
Whether by shorter route or greater,
I will get there, late or later.

One foot,
                two foot,
three foot,
                four . . .

That's what it takes,
                just that, no more.

Lizard

Still as a root
      I cling to the rock face, warmed by the sun,
          or lie on the sand like a brittle gray twig . . .

          and then

A shadow passes—

          Zip! I'm gone.

Where do I go?
      Oh, I'll find a crack in the friendly earth,
          or else a chink in a welcoming rock . . .
             there's always a sliver of dark somewhere . . .

    Then out I creep, into glare and heat
          to wait . . . and wait . . .

        until

A fly comes my way—

          Snap! It's gone.

Butterfly

flitterly flutterly

zippily zuppily

fluterly flittily

piffily puffily

Is my rhyme and reason
simply to flutter-by
all the warm season—
being a butterfly?

I may seem to cover
no distance at all,
haphazardly hover
from spring until fall,

but looks are deceiving.
I'm busy all day—
and soon I'll be leaving
for shores far away.

Though fragile as petals,
my wings are so strong
they take me on travels
incredibly long!

flutterly flittily

zuppily zippily

puffily

piffily

flitterly

flutter—

Bison

Solid I stand on the treeless plain,

heavy as hills,

patient as stone.

Here I will stand till the year comes around.

But that can all change.

In an eyeblink—I'm off!

And so are the others, sisters and brothers,

aunts and uncles and dozens of cousins,

hundreds and thousands of galloping cousins—

off we all go, every last one!

Rousing the world by our boisterous passing,

tromping to tatters the tall prairie grasses,

pounding the earth till the dust meets the clouds—

and a rumble like thunder rolls through the ground!

But every commotion must come to an end . . .

I stop,

and stamp,

and stand again.

Elk

Let others gallop, dash and leap,

flutter and skulk,

scurry and prowl—

my life by dignified measure proceeds!

I make my rounds with unhurried tread,

keep my own pace, command my space—

for I am sovereign here.

But if run I must, then

run I will—

and none can run with a grander gait . . .

a regal prance,

but swift and straight.

Let no one doubt

who is sovereign here!

Bear Print

A bear came here,
a bear went there,
and left no trace
of hide or hair.

> Where am I now,
> that mighty bear?
> Too shy to creep
> outside my lair?

Too sleepy still
for sunlight's glare—
too lazy for
life's wear and tear?

> No, I'm around,
> this morning rare,
> but hungry as—
> a bear, I swear!

So I have come
and gone somewhere
to see about
my breakfast fare.

> And that is why
> I'm on my way,
> leaving just
> one sign to say . . .

A bear came here,
a bear went there,
and all that shows
is paw of bear.

Deer

Head high, hard-pressed,
    I clear the windfall—
        bound over boulder
    splash along creek
  from thicket and woods to open field,
       leaping at random just beyond grasp—

until at last I leave danger behind.

Midst tall dry grass I pick my way
and browse the withering leaves,
in mottled shade find a moment's rest . . .

yet always ready to leap once more
    through autumn rains and winter drifts,
    greening spring and summer's haze . . .

always aware I'm in someone's eye.

Rabbit

When the moon is high
and the night is still,
I dance feather-footedly over the hill.

For a nibble or two
I can make some stops—
then on with the dancing, the bounces and hops!

But when day is bright,
others' eyes are keen—
my capers are hardly a sight to be seen!

Warily poised,
watching aquiver,
shivering whiskers—
Oh! in a dither
I zig and I zag,
and off in a flurry!
Now here, now there,
I scamper and scurry

till the dark returns
and everything's still . . .
and once more I'll dance on the crest of the hill.

Dog

Sometimes I long
  to run without hold,
  to lope and dash and lollop and trot . . .
      never to tire from first light till last,
  with the wind in my ears,
          wind of far places,
              songs of beyond.

I would run to the ends of the earth
if I could—

but I measure my steps by another's pace.
Close to the heel, consenting, I stay.

It's not just the fire that comforts my limbs—
a deeper warmth kindles my heart.
Another's voice gives me my name,
a hand reminds me of who I am . . .
          and the sounds in my ears
              are songs of belonging,
              songs of my home.

Handprint

Here I am!
Man
Woman
Child
Here we are!

Not so fleet as deer
    or strong as bison
    stealthy as lion
    or nimble as sheep . . .
Not so patient as turtle
    or noble as elk
    supple as snake
    or mobile as duck . . .
Not so snappy as lizard
    persistent as butterfly
    agile as rabbit
    or steady as dog . . .

But here we are—
man woman child—
to work, to dance,
create and love . . .
to care for this home,
gift to us all.

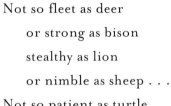

Notes

Snake

In traditional Native American cultures, snakes were revered. The snake's ability to disappear quickly into holes and clefts in rock suggested that it could enter the underworld and serve as a messenger between the everyday world and that of the spirits. In rock art, snakes often appear close to shamanic figures, perhaps helping in the shamans' spiritual travels. Snake images may have had other beneficial meanings as well, associated with water, fertility, and rejuvenation. Snakes are usually depicted in two different ways: a long zigzag line, sometimes with a small head at one end, or a spiral.

In nature, snakes move forward by a series of sideways loops, made by contracting and relaxing sets of muscles on each side. The snake's entire body, except for its head, constantly touches the ground. The head is slightly raised as the snake looks around for pebbles, twigs, or clumps of grass to push against. (On a very smooth, slippery surface it can hardly move at all.) Depending on the species, snakes have up to 400 vertebrae, each with a set of ribs. The large, wide scales on the underside of the snake's body, beneath the ribs, catch on the ground and help to move the snake along.

How speedy is a snake? Some snakes can make quick motions when escaping from a threat or catching prey. In general, however, they are sluggish creatures who really prefer to spend their time resting. The snake's quiet behavior and unblinking eyes may help to explain why some people have attributed mystic powers to this intriguing animal.

Bighorn Sheep

Bighorn sheep are one of the most frequently depicted animals in Southwestern rock art. They come in many shapes and styles. Some have curving horns, some just "stick-horns"; some sheep are box-shaped, others have "half-moon" bodies; some appear to be running flat-out, others standing still; some have big feet, and some no feet at all. The various peoples who lived in the Southwest over thousands of years had different ways of representing this animal, evidently so important to them.

In some rock art panels, groups of bighorns appear with dogs and humanlike figures. These scenes may have been intended to bring success in the hunt, to record and give thanks for a good hunt, or possibly to ask for the goodwill of animals already killed.

Sheep images could have had other important meanings as well. In many traditional societies, horned animals are believed to possess special power. Bighorns, with their remarkably large, curving horns, seem to have been associated with rain. The killing of a sheep, with its blood flow, may have been part of rain-bringing rituals. Sheep are also frequently placed close to shamanic or other supernatural figures in rock art panels, perhaps as spirit helpers.

Amazing climbers, bighorns can scramble up almost vertical rock faces. Descending, they may leap as far as fifty feet at a time. Their hooves, with hard outer rims and a spongy inside, grip the rock and also provide firm footing on slippery, mossy surfaces. At two weeks old, lambs not only can keep up with their mothers, but play with other lambs—on perilously steep slopes. Once in a while, a sheep does slip and fall to its death.

Bighorns are social animals, living in herds and migrating seasonally. Although they can run rapidly for short distances, their main defense is to climb too high for predators to follow. That's why they prefer to live in rocky, rugged terrain, where the heights give them a good view of possible danger.

Duck

The modest duck may have been one of the most powerful of all the creatures depicted in Southwestern rock art, with a prominent role in shamanic activity. Humanlike figures that may represent shamans often are accompanied by ducks, which sometimes sit on the shaman's head or even replace it. This could suggest that in his or her spiritual journey, the shaman used the duck's power to fly. Some Native American groups may have believed that the shaman actually became a duck to travel into the spirit world. In fact, the duck's ability to move in different ways—in the air, on land, and in water—may help explain its important role in shamanic magic.

Pueblo peoples' stories from the nineteenth and twentieth centuries hint at the possible meaning of these rock images. Because the duck migrates long distances by air, it is regarded as a traveler and messenger, a wise creature who has seen the world and knows a lot. A water-loving bird, it may carry messages to the clouds, asking them to produce rain. The duck also seems to have powers for healing.

Paddling with its webbed feet as it floats on the water, a duck looks perfectly at home. Then it may dive to the bottom of the pond in search of food. Some species dive as deep as forty feet—and some, with the help of a little wing power, can run across the surface of water. On land, the duck looks less at ease, but it can rush speedily for short distances. When it wants to become airborne, the duck can rise straight up—which can help in escaping a predator's pounce. At migration time, it may fly a thousand miles or more. A versatile creature indeed!

Mountain Lion

Some Native Americans call the mountain lion "ghost walker" because of its shy, stealthy ways. In rock art as in nature, mountain lion images are relatively rare. When they do appear, however—usually with a lean body, four large paws with claws, a mouth full of teeth, and a long tail—they are often striking.

In spite of the mountain lion's elusiveness, it appears to have been important in traditional Indian beliefs. As a spirit helper, it aided men in their search for large game and possibly also in warfare. It had curative powers as well, helping victims of disease and hunting injuries.

A solitary animal, the mountain lion avoids the territory of other lions. It can live in any terrain from swamp to mountaintop and is the only predator that can pursue the bighorn sheep to high peaks. Built for the hunt, the lion can travel twenty-five to thirty miles in a day. The thick fur on its paws allows it to run almost silently, while strong hind legs give it a powerful push in leaping. In fact, the lion can leap thirty feet in a single bound, jump sixteen to eighteen feet up into a tree, and drop safely sixty-five feet—as if from a five-story building.

When stalking, the mountain lion crouches close to the ground and moves inch by inch, seeming as motionless as a fallen tree. Then, when near enough, it leaps upon its victim in one or two bounds. Sometimes it has to chase its prey, running smoothly and with agility, its long tail helping it keep balance while making rapid sharp turns. Even with its strength and speed, however, the fearsome lion does not always win the race.

Turtle

The turtle is a familiar figure in Southwestern Indian crafts and stories. In rock art, its image seems to be related to water and fertility—all-important aspects of desert life.

Turtles live in water, while their cousins the tortoises live on dry land. Although rock art images of these creatures are typically called "turtle," the tortoise will be described here, because it is more likely to be found in desert country. A tortoise is indeed a slow walker, taking up to five hours to travel a mile. That's all right with the tortoise, though: it's a plant-eater and doesn't have to catch prey. Its shell provides a movable house—and fort. If a coyote, badger, or eagle comes after a tortoise, it can simply shut down, drawing head, legs, and tail inside its shell. A female tortoise does the same to discourage an unwelcome suitor.

Because daily extremes in temperature are typical of the desert environment, the tortoise, like all reptiles, has to avoid getting either too hot or too cold. Some kinds go underground, using their strong, thick legs to dig tunnels that may extend as far as forty feet. Here the tortoise can find shelter from the desert sun—and enjoy the company of various other small creatures who may move in to escape the heat of day and cold of night. With its quiet ways, the tortoise is a good neighbor.

Lizard

In Zuni stories, human beings had tails "at the time of the beginning." This connection between people and lizardlike creatures may help explain the many rock art images that look partly like humans with splayed arms and legs, and partly like lizards with short tails. Lizards in Southwestern rock art may also be related to the activities of shamans. Like snakes, lizards can disappear quickly into openings in rock or earth, which gives rise to the idea that they could be messengers between this world and that of the spirits.

Anyone who has seen a small lizard knows how fast these creatures can run, their legs barely skimming the ground. The common gecko can scurry up vertical walls and even along ceilings. On the underside of its toes are extremely small hooks that catch onto the slightest roughness in a surface. Some lizards, however, move in other ways—strutting stiff-legged to scare off an attacker, for instance. A horned toad (really a lizard) creeps silently toward a small insect and suddenly shoots out a long tongue to catch its prey. The Gila monster is too heavy and sluggish to move fast at all, so it seeks such prey as eggs and baby birds.

Even the most nimble lizard can get caught. But it may escape, thanks to its ability to shed part of its tail. Then it usually grows another, shorter tail. This could be why the lizard seems to have yet another meaning in Native American rock art and stories. It may symbolize rejuvenation: the idea that the body can be renewed after injury, or perhaps even after death.

Butterfly

The butterfly, although not a common image at rock art sites, comes in a variety of forms. Some images appear to be just two blob-shaped wings; yet the figure makes us immediately think "butterfly." Other figures identified as butterflies are symmetrical geometric forms, while a certain Hopi clan symbol is unmistakably a butterfly. This creature may be associated with rain, fertility, and well-being. According to one legend, the Creator brought butterflies into the world by asking the South Wind to breathe life into colored stones in a stream.

The butterfly's life history certainly inspires imagination. As a caterpillar, it starts out with many pairs of short legs and eventually wraps itself up in a cocoon. Later, when the butterfly emerges, its many short legs have changed into three pairs of long, delicate ones capable only of resting or walking lightly. It is now a creature of the air, with two sets of wings. Depending largely on the shape of the wings, different kinds of butterflies fly in different ways. They flap, flutter, float, dart, glide, hover. To keep its body at the right temperature, a butterfly moves frequently between sun and shade. Because butterflies have little defense against predators (birds, lizards, even cows), they must try to escape from danger. Some can fly rapidly, and others zigzag in and out among grasses and leaves.

Probably the most surprising thing about butterflies is their remarkable strength. Several kinds migrate south a few hundred miles to escape cold weather. The monarch butterfly, however, can fly up to 3,000 miles to its wintering place in Mexico—and then make the return trip north in the spring!

Bison

The bison, or buffalo as it is usually called in North America, is a latecomer in Southwestern rock art, attributed mostly to Utes and Navajos from the sixteenth through nineteenth centuries. Since bison are not normally found in desert and canyon country, their images may not have had the same sort of spiritual or magical qualities as those of some other animals. Perhaps these bison figures, typically small but often quite realistic, express awe and respect for a mighty creature—as well as hopes for good hunting.

The largest land animal in North America, the male bison can measure about six feet tall and twelve feet long, and weigh a ton or more. In spite of its bulk, a bison can run as fast as a horse. In the past, when bison herds lived on open plains with no place to hide, they had to be long-distance, speedy runners with the stamina to outlast attacking wolves. The massive hump and front quarters of the animal help it to run quickly, while its slim hind legs allow it to stop and turn in an instant.

Bison are moody and unpredictable. Although they usually appear calm and in no hurry to go anywhere, they may suddenly start to run. They run and run and run—and then stop! And then, for no apparent reason, they may turn and run in a different direction. Because of the bison's stampeding instinct, Indians on the Great Plains could force whole herds to run into corrals or over cliffs, where they could easily be killed.

Elk

Elk—or deer? Both are numerous in the Southwest, both were important game animals for Native Americans, and in rock art their images look much alike. We can, however, see some differences. In general, the larger the figure, the heavier or more blocklike its body, the more upright its head, and above all, the more impressive its antlers, the more likely it is to be an elk image, rather than a deer.

Elk often appear in rock art panels with images of other game animals and sometimes with hunters holding bows and arrows. In some figures, an arrow or spear appears to have pierced the animal's body. It seems that elk were depicted primarily in connection with hunting.

The male elk does have an air of being "king of the forest." In spring and summer, while his new set of broad, graceful antlers is growing, the male keeps to himself. By September, if sufficiently strong and persistent, he will win for himself a collection of female elk. His interest in domestic life soon wanes, however, and he goes off to spend the winter with other "bachelors."

Elk can run fast, with long, smooth strides. Males, with a top speed of thirty-five miles per hour, can outrun timber wolves, and females may gang up to chase a marauding coyote. But they run only when necessary. Elk can also jump, but only as high as necessary. They swim, and swim well . . . when necessary. Evidently, elk see little sense in exerting themselves. A healthy bull elk, with plenty to eat and with few predators foolish enough to come after him, can indeed lead a life of dignified leisure.

Bear

Like many traditional societies the world over, Native Americans have long considered the bear a potent symbol of strength and intelligence, with power both on earth and in the supernatural world. Among Pueblo Indians, for instance, the bear was especially revered. In addition to having knowledge of medicine and the ability to cure illness, it was thought to have powers that could counteract the evil of witches. Some tribes attributed shamanistic qualities to the bear, regarding it as the shaman's assistant or a guardian that helped the shaman confront malevolent beings.

These powers help explain the importance of bear footprints in Southwestern rock art, especially as clan symbols. Although entire figures of bears appear at various sites, the footprint evidently was thought to have particular potency. Images of bear footprints and human footprints look quite similar, aside from the bear's five long claws.

In nature, the bear is considered the strongest of North American land animals. Despite its bulky appearance and the turned-in position of its front feet, it can run fast: up to twenty-five miles per hour for short distances. Yet when attacked, it stands its ground with stamina and courage.

We humans tend to feel a special relationship with bears—possibly because, in some ways, bears look like people. A bear's skeleton is surprisingly like that of humans. The foot is flat, like our feet, and the hind legs bend forward, with kneecaps like ours. When a bear stands upright, as it does often, its back is straight and its head erect, the forepaws hanging loosely from sloping "shoulders." Moreover, bears have a wise, knowing look, and their behavior often suggests a curiosity about their surroundings. Small wonder that the bear has such a prominent place in Native American cultures!

Deer

Like bighorns, deer appear often in the rock art of the Southwest. Numerous panels show hunting scenes in which deer are the target, some pierced by arrows or spears. Native Americans of the past also seem to have regarded deer as spirit helpers that could assist shamans with weather control, fertility, and the curing of illness. In the Pueblo belief system, the blood flow from killing deer was associated with the idea of bringing rain.

The deer in nature is the favorite food of many predators. Camouflaged by its tawny coat, it can often keep safe by standing perfectly still. But a deer is also an escape artist. With a long, slim body, it can easily run through woods and brush. Its light but strong bones and powerful muscles are made for a life of speed—up to thirty-five miles per hour. Running on the tips of the two pointed toes that form each hoof, the deer is very agile, able to start, stop, and change direction instantly. A spectacular jumping machine as well, a deer can cover fifteen to twenty feet in a single graceful leap and clear heights of up to eight feet. With those long, seemingly delicate legs, it can even swim well.

The kind of deer most common in the Southwest is the mule deer, so called because of its large, mule-like ears. While the white-tailed deer runs with a smooth gait, the mule deer tends to run stiff-legged, bounding along with all four hooves off the ground at the same time. This gait helps it zigzag quickly on mountainous terrain to elude a pursuing wolf or mountain lion.

Rabbit

Rabbits live everywhere, from snowy plains to desert rocks. With their charming, gentle appearance, they have a special appeal for humans. But to most of a rabbit's neighbors—hawks, coyotes, snakes—it looks like one thing: good food. A rabbit's life focuses on eating and escaping.

Rabbits often stand tall on their hind legs to listen and look for danger. If caught in the open, a rabbit's first line of defense is to "freeze" and blend in with the surrounding grass or brush. Then it may have to run for its life. But as it cannot run fast for long, it must evade its pursuer by rapidly changing its course, zigzagging in a seemingly random way to confuse and tire the fox or bobcat on its tail.

Strong hind legs give the rabbit power to push off the ground and change direction. Most rabbits move in hops, covering distances of ten feet or more in a single leap. The rabbit's cousin, the hare (jackrabbits are really hares), can run with speed. When being pursued, it often jumps straight up to see where its enemy is.

Do rabbits actually dance? People sometimes see rabbits "dancing" in the moonlight. These rabbits are probably courting, the male trying to attract the female by hopping around her until she joins in the dance and hops along with him.

Surprisingly, although common in the ecology of the Southwest, rabbits and hares appear only rarely in rock art. Perhaps they were not considered important as links between humans and the spirit world. If that is so, it may confirm the special significance of those animals that were frequently depicted—and the much deeper meaning of animal images than simply a record of the environment.

Dog

Some 8,500 years ago, three dogs in an Indian settlement in Illinois were given careful burials. Their graves, discovered by twentieth-century archaeologists, are proof of dogs' long friendship with humans.

That relationship comes across in rock art. At some sites, dogs appear with bighorn sheep and humanlike figures, evidently as part of hunting expeditions. But they seem to have had a more spiritual role as well. Like certain other animals, they were placed close to figures that may represent shamans or spirits. It looks as though the dogs served as important helpers or messengers, accompanying shamans into the spirit world—much as dogs walk with and protect people today.

The "spirit dogs," with solid, chunky bodies that look quite huggable, appear to be quiet and gentle. In this world, however, the dog is made for action. Most dogs can run fast in short spurts, but their real strength lies in stamina—the energy to lope at a steady pace for long distances. Their endurance and patience are essential in hunting. Dogs' flexible joints and sturdy limbs give them excellent stability while running. Agile as well, some kinds of dogs can leap several times their own height. Powerful hindquarters give them spring, and strong shoulder muscles help them to land safely, with pads on the forefeet for a good grip.

Dogs owe their success as a species not just to their physical qualities, but also to their social nature. They form friendly relationships with other dogs—and, of course, with us.

Human Handprint

Of all the creatures in Southwestern rock art, one kind appears most often: human beings. They take many forms. Most are "sort-of-human" beings: tall, elegant, ghostlike shapes; spidery, wispy images; solid, blocklike forms with tiny limbs; or stick figures. But portrayals of nineteenth-century Mexican soldiers also turn up on rock faces! These widely varying humanlike images must have held many different meanings for those who made them.

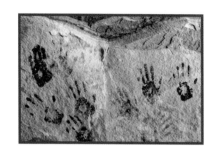

Yet one form of human representation appears over and over again: handprints. In rock art, handprints are usually pictographs (made with paint). At some sites, the hand was smeared with color and pressed onto the rock face. Other prints were made by holding the hand against the wall and blowing pigment around it through a short tube such as a hollow reed, creating a negative image.

What could a handprint mean? Possibly it was an affirmation of a prayer or ritual, or perhaps a claim to a certain place—or maybe something altogether different. We can only guess. But these handprints at sites throughout the Southwest show us one thing clearly: the emphatic presence of human beings, big and little, old and young. We were here!

While we humans don't move around much on our hands, of course, there is a connection between hands and the ways we move. Our unique ability to use our thumbs and fingers to hold things—as large as a log or tiny as a grain of sand—helps us to explore the world, to make and manipulate. That ability leads us to excel in something that animals can do only to a very limited extent. We think: we reason, solve problems, create, remember.

Because we can decide to do many different things, we move our bodies in extraordinarily varied ways. Our arched foot enables us to stand upright and keep our balance, absorbing shock as we move. Our joints work in different ways: the knee joint moves back and forth, while the hip joint can move in several directions. Thus we can dance and swim, skip with happiness, climb sheer cliffsides, and strut with pride. We can dash and dawdle, leap and lope, skate and scuttle; we can crawl across a floor, trudge across a sand dune, and stand on one foot for hours. We can move our bodies almost any way we wish.

Humans are not, however, "running machines." Even the fastest runners can reach only about twenty-two miles per hour, for very short distances. Since ordinarily we cannot outrun danger or run down our prey, we have to rely on our brains to get what we want. We often leave a mark to show others that we have succeeded, or to convey some other information. And that's where, in Southwestern rock art, the handprint comes in. Although it may originally have been intended as a communication with the spirits, today the handprint connects with us. It offers an intimate greeting in a vast world, through the ages. *We were here, as you can see. We were here, living our lives the best we could.*